Philippa Nikulinsky was born in Kalgoorlie, Western Australia, in 1942. She trained as an art teacher and has taught in a number of secondary schools and tertiary institutions. She now works full-time as a natural history artist and illustrator, specialising in Australian native flora.

Philippa Nikulinsky's work has appeared in numerous group and solo exhibitions throughout Australia, and she has received many major public and corporate commissions in Australia and overseas. Her work has also been included in a wide variety of books and journals. She has previously published three books — *Western Australian Wildflowers in Watercolour, Banksia Menziesii* (both published by Fremantle Arts Centre Press) and *Flowering Plants of the Eastern Goldfields of Western Australia* — a limited edition of prints and a number of posters. Six previous diaries have also been published by Fremantle Arts Centre Press — *Australian Native Bird Diary 1994* and *Australian Wildflower Diary 1993, 1995, 1996, 1997 and 1998.*

First published 1998 by
FREMANTLE ARTS CENTRE PRESS
193 South Terrace (PO Box 320), South Fremantle
Western Australia 6162.
http://www.facp.iinet.net.au

Designed by John Douglass
Production Coordinator Cate Sutherland

Typesetting by Fremantle Arts Centre Press
Scanning and film separations by Complete Imaging Centre
and printed by Sands Print Group, Western Australia.

ISBN 1 86368 231 7

PERSONAL MEMORANDA

PERSONAL

Name

Address

Telephone

Blood Group

Driving Licence No.

Passport No.

BUSINESS

Company

Address

Telephone

Facsimile

REMINDERS

Passport Renewal

Insurance Renewals

Driving Licence Renewal

Income Tax Return due

Medical Check-up

Dental Check-up

Vaccinations

Others

IMPORTANT TELEPHONE NUMBERS

Doctor

Dentist

Police

Ambulance

Fire Brigade

Bank

Solicitor

RAC

Taxi Service

Electricity

Gas

Plumber

Others

IMPORTANT DATES

Birthdays

Anniversaries

Social Events

Others

1999 CALENDAR

JANUARY

M	T	W	T	F	S	S
				1	2	3
4	5	6	7	8	9	10
11	12	13	14	15	16	17
18	19	20	21	22	23	24
25	26	27	28	29	30	31

FEBRUARY

M	T	W	T	F	S	S
1	2	3	4	5	6	7
8	9	10	11	12	13	14
15	16	17	18	19	20	21
22	23	24	25	26	27	28

MARCH

M	T	W	T	F	S	S
1	2	3	4	5	6	7
8	9	10	11	12	13	14
15	16	17	18	19	20	21
22	23	24	25	26	27	28
29	30	31				

APRIL

M	T	W	T	F	S	S
			1	2	3	4
5	6	7	8	9	10	11
12	13	14	15	16	17	18
19	20	21	22	23	24	25
26	27	28	29	30		

MAY

M	T	W	T	F	S	S
					1	2
3	4	5	6	7	8	9
10	11	12	13	14	15	16
17	18	19	20	21	22	23
24	25	26	27	28	29	30
31						

JUNE

M	T	W	T	F	S	S
	1	2	3	4	5	6
7	8	9	10	11	12	13
14	15	16	17	18	19	20
21	22	23	24	25	26	27
28	29	30				

JULY

M	T	W	T	F	S	S
			1	2	3	4
5	6	7	8	9	10	11
12	13	14	15	16	17	18
19	20	21	22	23	24	25
26	27	28	29	30	31	

AUGUST

M	T	W	T	F	S	S
						1
2	3	4	5	6	7	8
9	10	11	12	13	14	15
16	17	18	19	20	21	22
23	24	25	26	27	28	29
30	31					

SEPTEMBER

M	T	W	T	F	S	S
		1	2	3	4	5
6	7	8	9	10	11	12
13	14	15	16	17	18	19
20	21	22	23	24	25	26
27	28	29	30			

OCTOBER

M	T	W	T	F	S	S
				1	2	3
4	5	6	7	8	9	10
11	12	13	14	15	16	17
18	19	20	21	22	23	24
25	26	27	28	29	30	31

NOVEMBER

M	T	W	T	F	S	S
1	2	3	4	5	6	7
8	9	10	11	12	13	14
15	16	17	18	19	20	21
22	23	24	25	26	27	28
29	30					

DECEMBER

M	T	W	T	F	S	S
		1	2	3	4	5
6	7	8	9	10	11	12
13	14	15	16	17	18	19
20	21	22	23	24	25	26
27	28	29	30	31		

PUBLIC HOLIDAYS & SCHOOL TERMS 1999

NATIONAL

New Year's Day . . . . 1 January
Australia Day . . . . 26 January
Good Friday . . . . 2 April
Easter Monday . . . . 5 April
Queen's Birthday . . . . 14 June*

ACT

Term 1 . . . . 2 February – 1 April
Term 2 . . . . 19 April – 2 July
Term 3 . . . . 19 July – 24 September
Term 4 . . . . 11 October – 17 December

Canberra Day . . . . 16 March
Anzac Day . . . . 25 April
Labour Day . . . . 5 October
Christmas Day . . . . 27 December
Boxing Day . . . . 28 December

NEW SOUTH WALES

Term 1 . . . . 27 January – 1 April**
                3 February – 1 April
Term 2 . . . . 19 April – 2 July
Term 3 . . . . 19 July – 24 September
Term 4 . . . . 11 October – 17 December

Bank Holiday . . . . 2 August
Anzac Day . . . . 26 April
Labour Day . . . . 4 October
Christmas Day . . . . 25 December
Boxing Day . . . . 27 December

NORTHERN TERRITORY

Term 1 . . . . 2 February – 9 April
Term 2 . . . . 19 April – 25 June
Term 3 . . . . 26 July – 1 October
Term 4 . . . . 11 October – 17 December

Anzac Day . . . . 26 April
May Day . . . . 3 May
Picnic Day . . . . 2 August
Christmas Day . . . . 27 December
Boxing Day . . . . 28 December

QUEENSLAND

Term 1 . . . . 25 January – 1 April
Term 2 . . . . 12 April – 18 June
Term 3 . . . . 6 July – 17 September
Term 4 . . . . 4 October – 17 December

Anzac Day . . . . 26 April
Labour Day . . . . 3 May
Brisbane Show Day . . . . . 11 August***
Christmas Day . . . . 25 December
Boxing Day . . . . 27 December

SOUTH AUSTRALIA

Term 1 . . . . 27 January – 1 April
Term 2 . . . . 19 April – 2 July
Term 3 . . . . 19 July – 24 September
Term 4 . . . . 11 October – 17 December

Anzac Day . . . . 26 April
Adelaide Cup . . . . 17 May
Labour Day . . . . 4 October
Christmas Day . . . . 27 December
Proclamation Day . . . . 28 December

TASMANIA

Term 1 . . . . 11 February – 28 May
Term 2 . . . . 15 June – 3 September
Term 3 . . . . 20 September – 17 December

Royal Hobart Regatta . . . . 9 February***
Eight Hours Day . . . . 1 March
Bank Holiday . . . . 6 April
Anzac Day . . . . 25 April
Hobart Show Day . . . . . . 21 October***
Christmas Day . . . . 27 December
Boxing Day . . . . 28 December

VICTORIA

Term 1 . . . . 27 January – 1 April
Term 2 . . . . 19 April – 25 June
Term 3 . . . . 27 July – 17 September
Term 4 . . . . 4 October – 17 December

Labour Day . . . . 8 March
Anzac Day . . . . 25 April
Melbourne Cup Day . . . . 3 November***
Christmas Day . . . . 25 December
Boxing Day . . . . 27 December

WESTERN AUSTRALIA

Term 1 . . . . 27 January – 1 April
Term 2 . . . . 19 April – 2 July
Term 3 . . . . 19 July – 24 September
Term 4 . . . . 11 October – 17 December

Labour Day . . . . 1 March
Anzac Day . . . . 26 April
Foundation Day . . . . 7 June
Queen's Birthday . . . . 27 September
Christmas Day . . . . 27 December
Boxing Day . . . . 28 December

*Except Western Australia
**First date is for Eastern Division schools, second
date for Western Division schools in New South Wales.
***Local holiday only.
NB: These dates may be subject to change.

1999 YEAR PLANNER

	January	February	March	April	May	June
Mon		1	1			
Tue		2	2			1
Wed		3	3			2
Thu		4	4	1		3
Fri	1	5	5	2		4
Sat	2	6	6	3	1	5
Sun	3	7	7	4	2	6
Mon	4	8	8	5	3	7
Tue	5	9	9	6	4	8
Wed	6	10	10	7	5	9
Thu	7	11	11	8	6	10
Fri	8	12	12	9	7	11
Sat	9	13	13	10	8	12
Sun	10	14	14	11	9	13
Mon	11	15	15	12	10	14
Tue	12	16	16	13	11	15
Wed	13	17	17	14	12	16
Thu	14	18	18	15	13	17
Fri	15	19	19	16	14	18
Sat	16	20	20	17	15	19
Sun	17	21	21	18	16	20
Mon	18	22	22	19	17	21
Tue	19	23	23	20	18	22
Wed	20	24	24	21	19	23
Thu	21	25	25	22	20	24
Fri	22	26	26	23	21	25
Sat	23	27	27	24	22	26
Sun	24	28	28	25	23	27
Mon	25		29	26	24	28
Tue	26		30	27	25	29
Wed	27		31	28	26	30
Thu	28			29	27	
Fri	29			30	28	
Sat	30				29	
Sun	31				30	
Mon					31	
Tue						

	January	February	March	April	May	June

1999 YEAR PLANNER

July	August	September	October	November	December	
				1		Mon
				2		Tue
		1		3	1	Wed
1		2		4	2	Thu
2		3	1	5	3	Fri
3		4	2	6	4	Sat
4	1	5	3	7	5	Sun
5	2	6	4	8	6	Mon
6	3	7	5	9	7	Tue
7	4	8	6	10	8	Wed
8	5	9	7	11	9	Thu
9	6	10	8	12	10	Fri
10	7	11	9	13	11	Sat
11	8	12	10	14	12	Sun
12	9	13	11	15	13	Mon
13	10	14	12	16	14	Tue
14	11	15	13	17	15	Wed
15	12	16	14	18	16	Thu
16	13	17	15	19	17	Fri
17	14	18	16	20	18	Sat
18	15	19	17	21	19	Sun
19	16	20	18	22	20	Mon
20	17	21	19	23	21	Tue
21	18	22	20	24	22	Wed
22	19	23	21	25	23	Thu
23	20	24	22	26	24	Fri
24	21	25	23	27	25	Sat
25	22	26	24	28	26	Sun
26	23	27	25	29	27	Mon
27	24	28	26	30	28	Tue
28	25	29	27		29	Wed
29	26	30	28		30	Thu
30	27		29		31	Fri
31	28		30			Sat
	29		31			Sun
	30					Mon
	31					Tue

July	August	September	October	November	December

JANUARY

M	T	W	T	F	S	S
				1	2	3
4	5	6	7	8	9	10
11	12	13	14	15	16	17
18	19	20	21	22	23	24
25	26	27	28	29	30	31

SLENDER BANKSIA
Banksia attenuata
Common between Kalbarri, Augusta and the Fitzgerald River in the south-west of
Western Australia.
Flowers late spring and summer.

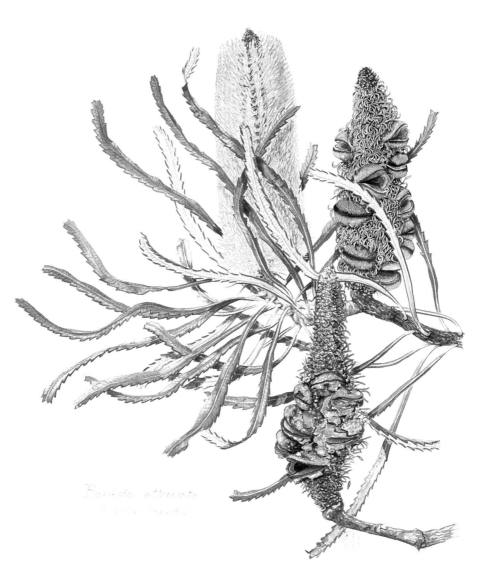

Banksia attenuata

28 MON DECEMBER

29 TUE DECEMBER

30 WED DECEMBER

31 THU DECEMBER

JANUARY FRI **1**

JANUARY SAT **2**

JANUARY SUN **3**

NOTES

4 MON JANUARY

5 TUE JANUARY

6 WED JANUARY

7 THU JANUARY

JANUARY FRI **8**

JANUARY SAT **9**

JANUARY SUN **10**

NOTES

JANUARY

M	T	W	T	F	S	S
				1	2	3
4	5	6	7	8	9	10
11	12	13	14	15	16	17
18	19	20	21	22	23	24
25	26	27	28	29	30	31

CORAL GUM
Eucalyptus torquata
Rather uncommon in the Eastern Goldfields of Western Australia, but widely cultivated.
Flowers winter and spring.

Philippa N Rutherbury 97   Eucalyptus torquata
                                            Coral Gum

11 MON JANUARY

12 TUE JANUARY

13 WED JANUARY

14 THU JANUARY

JANUARY FRI **15**

JANUARY SAT **16**

JANUARY SUN **17**

NOTES

18 MON JANUARY

19 TUE JANUARY

20 WED JANUARY

21 THU JANUARY

NOTES

JANUARY

M	T	W	T	F	S	S
				1	2	3
4	5	6	7	8	9	10
11	12	13	14	15	16	17
18	19	20	21	22	23	24
25	26	27	28	29	30	31

STURT PEA
Swainsona formosa
Widespread in arid Australia. Floral emblem of South Australia.
Flowers mainly winter and spring.

Swainsona formosa
(*Clianthus formosus*)
Sturt's Desert Pea

Philippa Nikulinsky

25 MON JANUARY

26 TUE JANUARY

27 WED JANUARY

28 THU JANUARY

JANUARY FRI **29**

JANUARY SAT **30**

JANUARY SUN 3**1**

NOTES

1 MON FEBRUARY

2 TUE FEBRUARY

3 WED FEBRUARY

4 THU FEBRUARY

NOTES

FEBRUARY

M	T	W	T	F	S	S
1	2	3	4	5	6	7
8	9	10	11	12	13	14
15	16	17	18	19	20	21
22	23	24	25	26	27	28

YELLOW LESCHENAULTIA
Lechenaultia linarioides
Occurs near the coast from Dirk Hartog Island to Perth, Western Australia.
Flowers sporadically, but mainly winter and spring.

Lechenaultia linarioides
'tangled lechenaultia'

Philippa Nikulinsky.

8 MON FEBRUARY

9 TUE FEBRUARY

10 WED FEBRUARY

11 THU FEBRUARY

FEBRUARY FRI 12

FEBRUARY SAT 13

FEBRUARY SUN 14

NOTES

15 MON FEBRUARY

16 TUE FEBRUARY

17 WED FEBRUARY

18 THU FEBRUARY

FEBRUARY FRI 19

FEBRUARY SAT 20

FEBRUARY SUN 21

NOTES

FEBRUARY

M	T	W	T	F	S	S
1	2	3	4	5	6	7
8	9	10	11	12	13	14
15	16	17	18	19	20	21
22	23	24	25	26	27	28

HAIRY LESCHENAULTIA
Lechenaultia hirsuta
Grows between Shark Bay and Jurien, Western Australia.
Flowers spring.

Lechenaultia hirsuta
Hairy Lechenaultia

Philippa Nikulinsky '98

22 MON FEBRUARY

23 TUE FEBRUARY

24 WED FEBRUARY

25 THU FEBRUARY

FEBRUARY FRI **26**

FEBRUARY SAT **27**

FEBRUARY SUN **28**

NOTES

1 MON MARCH

2 TUE MARCH

3 WED MARCH

4 THU MARCH

MARCH FRI 5

MARCH SAT 6

MARCH SUN 7

NOTES

MARCH

M	T	W	T	F	S	S
1	2	3	4	5	6	7
8	9	10	11	12	13	14
15	16	17	18	19	20	21
22	23	24	25	26	27	28
29	30	31				

BALD ISLAND MARLOCK
Eucalyptus conferruminata
Occurs between Two Peoples Bay and Esperance, including islands, Western Australia.
Flowers mainly winter and spring.

Eucalyptus conferruminata
Bald Island marlock

Philippa N Rutnisky '97

8 MON MARCH

9 TUE MARCH

10 WED MARCH

11 THU MARCH

NOTES

15 MON MARCH

16 TUE MARCH

17 WED MARCH

18 THU MARCH

MARCH FRI **19**

MARCH SAT **20**

MARCH SUN **21**

NOTES

MARCH

M	T	W	T	F	S	S
1	2	3	4	5	6	7
8	9	10	11	12	13	14
15	16	17	18	19	20	21
22	23	24	25	26	27	28
29	30	31				

SILVER PRINCESS
Eucalyptus caesia subsp. *magna*
Grows on a few granite rocks in the inland south-west of
Western Australia, but widely grown in gardens.
Flowers autumn and winter.

Eucalyptus caesia subsp. magna
Silver Princess

Philippa Nikulinsky

22 MON MARCH

23 TUE MARCH

24 WED MARCH

25 THU MARCH

MARCH FRI **26**

MARCH SAT **27**

MARCH SUN **28**

NOTES

29 MON MARCH

30 TUE MARCH

31 WED MARCH

1 THU APRIL

APRIL FRI **2**

APRIL SAT **3**

APRIL SUN **4**

NOTES

APRIL

M	T	W	T	F	S	S
			1	2	3	4
5	6	7	8	9	10	11
12	13	14	15	16	17	18
19	20	21	22	23	24	25
26	27	28	29	30		

NATIVE FRANGIPANI
Hymenosporum flavum
A rainforest tree of north-eastern New South Wales, Queensland and New Guinea.
Flowers spring.

Hymenosporum flavum
Native Frangipani

Philippa Nikulinsky

5 MON APRIL

6 TUE APRIL

7 WED APRIL

8 THU APRIL

APRIL FRI 9

APRIL SAT 10

APRIL SUN 11

NOTES

12 MON APRIL

13 TUE APRIL

14 WED APRIL

15 THU APRIL

APRIL FRI **16**

APRIL SAT **17**

APRIL SUN **18**

NOTES

APRIL

M	T	W	T	F	S	S
			1	2	3	4
5	6	7	8	9	10	11
12	13	14	15	16	17	18
19	20	21	22	23	24	25
26	27	28	29	30		

YARDIE MORNING GLORY
Ipomoea yardiensis
An unusual shrubby morning glory, restricted to the Cape Range, Western Australia.
Flowers winter.

Ipomoea yardiensis
Yardie Morning-glory

Philippa Nikulinsky '97

19 MON APRIL

20 TUE APRIL

21 WED APRIL

22 THU APRIL

APRIL FRI **23**

APRIL SAT **24**

APRIL SUN **25**

NOTES

26 MON APRIL

27 TUE APRIL

28 WED APRIL

29 THU APRIL

MAY SAT **1**

MAY SUN **2**

NOTES

MAY

M	T	W	T	F	S	S
					1	2
3	4	5	6	7	8	9
10	11	12	13	14	15	16
17	18	19	20	21	22	23
24	25	26	27	28	29	30
31						

SHOWY BANKSIA
Banksia speciosa
Showy Banksia grows between Hopetoun and the western end of the
Great Australian Bight, Western Australia.
Flowers mainly summer and autumn.

NEW HOLLAND HONEYEATER
Phylidonyris novaehollandiae

3 MON MAY

4 TUE MAY

5 WED MAY

6 THU MAY

MAY FRI **7**

MAY SAT **8**

MAY SUN **9**

NOTES

10 MON MAY

11 TUE MAY

12 WED MAY

13 THU MAY

NOTES

MAY

M	T	W	T	F	S	S
					1	2
3	4	5	6	7	8	9
10	11	12	13	14	15	16
17	18	19	20	21	22	23
24	25	26	27	28	29	30
31						

GREEN CASSIA
Senna glutinosa subsp. *chatelainiana*
Green Cassia is common in the central west of Western Australia

HAIRY MULLA MULLA
Ptilotus helipteroides
Hairy Mulla Mulla is widespread in arid Western Australia and the Northern Territory.
Both flower winter and spring.

Cassia & Ptilotus

17 MON MAY

18 TUE MAY

19 WED MAY

20 THU MAY

MAY FRI **21**

MAY SAT **22**

MAY SUN **23**

NOTES

24 MON MAY

25 TUE MAY

26 WED MAY

27 THU MAY

MAY FRI 28

MAY SAT 29

MAY SUN 30

NOTES

MAY

M	T	W	T	F	S	S
					1	2
3	4	5	6	7	8	9
10	11	12	13	14	15	16
17	18	19	20	21	22	23
24	25	26	27	28	29	30
31						

POVERTY BUSH
Eremophila flaccida
A rather uncommon, sticky shrub of the southern
Pilbara, Western Australia.
Flowers winter.

Philippa Nikulinsky 97

31 MON MAY

1 TUE JUNE

2 WED JUNE

3 THU JUNE

JUNE FRI **4**

JUNE SAT **5**

JUNE SUN **6**

NOTES

7 MON JUNE

8 TUE JUNE

9 WED JUNE

10 THU JUNE

NOTES

JUNE

M	T	W	T	F	S	S
	1	2	3	4	5	6
7	8	9	10	11	12	13
14	15	16	17	18	19	20
21	22	23	24	25	26	27
28	29	30				

GRANITE BOTTLEBRUSH
Melaleuca elliptica
Common on inland granite rocks of south-western Australia.
Flowers winter and spring.

14 MON JUNE

15 TUE JUNE

16 WED JUNE

17 THU JUNE

JUNE FRI **18**

JUNE SAT **19**

JUNE SUN **20**

NOTES

21 MON JUNE

22 TUE JUNE

23 WED JUNE

24 THU JUNE

NOTES

JUNE

M	T	W	T	F	S	S
	1	2	3	4	5	6
7	8	9	10	11	12	13
14	15	16	17	18	19	20
21	22	23	24	25	26	27
28	29	30				

RAPIER FEATHERFLOWER
Verticordia mitchelliana
Occurs in the inland south-west of Western Australia.
Flowers spring.

Verticordia mitchelliana
Rapier featherflower

Philippa Nikulinsky

28 MON JUNE

29 TUE JUNE

30 WED JUNE

1 THU JULY

JULY FRI **2**

JULY SAT **3**

JULY SUN **4**

NOTES

5 MON JULY

6 TUE JULY

7 WED JULY

8 THU JULY

JULY FRI **9**

JULY SAT **10**

JULY SUN **11**

NOTES

JULY

M	T	W	T	F	S	S
			1	2	3	4
5	6	7	8	9	10	11
12	13	14	15	16	17	18
19	20	21	22	23	24	25
26	27	28	29	30	31	

RED ROD
Eremophila calorhabdos
Occurs in the Norseman area, Western Australia.
Flowers spring and early summer.

Eremophila calorhabdos

Philippa Nikulinsky

12 MON JULY

13 TUE JULY

14 WED JULY

15 THU JULY

JULY FRI 16

JULY SAT 17

JULY SUN 18

NOTES

19 MON JULY

20 TUE JULY

21 WED JULY

22 THU JULY

JULY FRI 23

JULY SAT 24

JULY SUN 25

NOTES

JULY

M	T	W	T	F	S	S
			1	2	3	4
5	6	7	8	9	10	11
12	13	14	15	16	17	18
19	20	21	22	23	24	25
26	27	28	29	30	31	

KAPOK BUSH
Cochlospermum fraseri subsp. *heteronemum*
Common in the Kimberley and the Top End of the Northern Territory.
Shown here in fruit, it has large yellow flowers in winter
and spring when it sheds its leaves.

Cochlospermum fraseri
Kapok bush

Philippa NiRulinsky

26 MON JULY

27 TUE JULY

28 WED JULY

29 THU JULY

JULY FRI **30**

JULY SAT 3**1**

AUGUST SUN **1**

NOTES

2 MON AUGUST

3 TUE AUGUST

4 WED AUGUST

5 THU AUGUST

AUGUST FRI 6

AUGUST SAT 7

AUGUST SUN 8

NOTES

AUGUST

M	T	W	T	F	S	S
						1
2	3	4	5	6	7	8
9	10	11	12	13	14	15
16	17	18	19	20	21	22
23	24	25	26	27	28	29
30	31					

THARGOMINDAH NIGHTSHADE
Solanum sturtianum
A wild tomato, common in arid regions of Australia.
Flowers winter and spring.

Solanum stuartianum
Wild tomato

Philippa Nikulinsky '97

9 MON AUGUST

10 TUE AUGUST

11 WED AUGUST

12 THU AUGUST

AUGUST FRI 13

AUGUST SAT 14

AUGUST SUN 15

NOTES

16 MON AUGUST

17 TUE AUGUST

18 WED AUGUST

19 THU AUGUST

AUGUST SAT **21**

AUGUST SUN **22**

NOTES

AUGUST

M	T	W	T	F	S	S
						1
2	3	4	5	6	7	8
9	10	11	12	13	14	15
16	17	18	19	20	21	22
23	24	25	26	27	28	29
30	31					

SWAMP ORCHID
Phaius tankervilliae
In Australia occurs from Cape York Peninsula to north-eastern New South Wales;
also through the islands north to south-east Asia, China and Japan.
Flowers spring.

Phaius tankervilleae.

Philippa Nikulinsky

23 MON AUGUST

24 TUE AUGUST

25 WED AUGUST

26 THU AUGUST

AUGUST FRI **27**

AUGUST SAT **28**

AUGUST SUN **29**

NOTES

30 MON AUGUST

31 TUE AUGUST

1 WED SEPTEMBER

2 THU SEPTEMBER

SEPTEMBER FRI **3**

SEPTEMBER SAT **4**

SEPTEMBER SUN **5**

NOTES

SEPTEMBER

M	T	W	T	F	S	S
			1	2	3	4	5
6	7	8	9	10	11	12
13	14	15	16	17	18	19
20	21	22	23	24	25	26
27	28	29	30			

WILD GERANIUM
Pelargonium drummondii
Grows on granite rocks in southern Western Australia.
Flowers spring and early summer.

Pelagonium

Philippe Kikulnsky

6 MON SEPTEMBER

7 TUE SEPTEMBER

8 WED SEPTEMBER

9 THU SEPTEMBER

SEPTEMBER FRI **10**

SEPTEMBER SAT **11**

SEPTEMBER SUN **12**

NOTES

13 MON SEPTEMBER

14 TUE SEPTEMBER

15 WED SEPTEMBER

16 THU SEPTEMBER

SEPTEMBER FRI **17**

SEPTEMBER SAT **18**

SEPTEMBER SUN **19**

NOTES

SEPTEMBER

M	T	W	T	F	S	S
		1	2	3	4	5
6	7	8	9	10	11	12
13	14	15	16	17	18	19
20	21	22	23	24	25	26
27	28	29	30			

YELLOW BELLS
Geleznowia verrucosa
Occurs between Shark Bay and Eneabba, Western Australia.
Flowers late winter and spring.

20 MON SEPTEMBER

21 TUE SEPTEMBER

22 WED SEPTEMBER

23 THU SEPTEMBER

SEPTEMBER FRI **24**

SEPTEMBER SAT **25**

SEPTEMBER SUN **26**

NOTES

27 MON SEPTEMBER

28 TUE SEPTEMBER

29 WED SEPTEMBER

30 THU SEPTEMBER

OCTOBER FRI **1**

OCTOBER SAT **2**

OCTOBER SUN **3**

NOTES

OCTOBER

M	T	W	T	F	S	S
				1	2	3
4	5	6	7	8	9	10
11	12	13	14	15	16	17
18	19	20	21	22	23	24
25	26	27	28	29	30	31

CONEBUSH
Petrophile teretifolia
Common from the Stirling Range to Israelite Bay, Western Australia.
Flowers spring.

Petrophile

Philippa Nikulinsky

4 MON OCTOBER

5 TUE OCTOBER

6 WED OCTOBER

7 THU OCTOBER

OCTOBER FRI **8**

OCTOBER SAT **9**

OCTOBER SUN **10**

NOTES

11 MON OCTOBER

12 TUE OCTOBER

13 WED OCTOBER

14 THU OCTOBER

OCTOBER FRI 15

OCTOBER SAT 16

OCTOBER SUN 17

NOTES

OCTOBER

M	T	W	T	F	S	S
				1	2	3
4	5	6	7	8	9	10
11	12	13	14	15	16	17
18	19	20	21	22	23	24
25	26	27	28	29	30	31

PINDAN WATTLE
Acacia tumida
A common wattle of the Kimberley and Top End of the Northern Territory.
Flowers winter.

Philippe Nikulinsky '90

18 MON OCTOBER

19 TUE OCTOBER

20 WED OCTOBER

21 THU OCTOBER

OCTOBER FRI 22

OCTOBER SAT 23

OCTOBER SUN 24

NOTES

25 MON OCTOBER

26 TUE OCTOBER

27 WED OCTOBER

28 THU OCTOBER

OCTOBER FRI 29

OCTOBER SAT 30

OCTOBER SUN 31

NOTES

NOVEMBER

M	T	W	T	F	S	S
1	2	3	4	5	6	7
8	9	10	11	12	13	14
15	16	17	18	19	20	21
22	23	24	25	26	27	28
29	30					

A SWAINSON PEA
Swainsona elegantoides
An annual vetch from the Gascoyne region and Little Sandy Desert, Western Australia.
Flowers late winter and early spring.

Swainsona

Philippa Nikulinsky 98

1 MON NOVEMBER

2 TUE NOVEMBER

3 WED NOVEMBER

4 THU NOVEMBER

NOTES

8 MON NOVEMBER

9 TUE NOVEMBER

10 WED NOVEMBER

11 THU NOVEMBER

NOVEMBER FRI **12**

NOVEMBER SAT **13**

NOVEMBER SUN **14**

NOTES

NOVEMBER

M	T	W	T	F	S	S
1	2	3	4	5	6	7
8	9	10	11	12	13	14
15	16	17	18	19	20	21
22	23	24	25	26	27	28
29	30					

LEAFLESS ORCHID
Caladenia aphylla
Common in the far south-west of Western Australia.
Flowers in autumn, when leafless.

Praecoxanthus aphyllus
Leafless Orchid

Philippa Nikulinsky

15 MON NOVEMBER

16 TUE NOVEMBER

17 WED NOVEMBER

18 THU NOVEMBER

NOVEMBER FRI **19**

NOVEMBER SAT **20**

NOVEMBER SUN **21**

NOTES

22 MON NOVEMBER

23 TUE NOVEMBER

24 WED NOVEMBER

25 THU NOVEMBER

NOVEMBER FRI **26**

NOVEMBER SAT **27**

NOVEMBER SUN **28**

NOTES

NOVEMBER

M	T	W	T	F	S	S
1	2	3	4	5	6	7
8	9	10	11	12	13	14
15	16	17	18	19	20	21
22	23	24	25	26	27	28
29	30					

STARFLOWER

Caltyrix carinata

A shrubby myrtle widespread in arid regions of subtropical Australia.
Flowers mainly winter.

29 MON NOVEMBER

30 TUE NOVEMBER

1 WED DECEMBER

2 THU DECEMBER

DECEMBER FRI 3

DECEMBER SAT 4

DECEMBER SUN 5

NOTES

6 MON DECEMBER

7 TUE DECEMBER

8 WED DECEMBER

9 THU DECEMBER

DECEMBER FRI **10**

DECEMBER SAT **11**

DECEMBER SUN **12**

NOTES

DECEMBER

M	T	W	T	F	S	S
			1	2	3	4	5
6	7	8	9	10	11	12
13	14	15	16	17	18	19
20	21	22	23	24	25	26
27	28	29	30	31		

RED LESCHENAULTIA
Lechenaultia formosa
Common in south-western Australia from Coorow to Israelite Bay.
Highly variable in flower colour.
Flowers mainly winter and spring

Lechenaultia formosa
Red lechenaultia

Philippa K. Pulinsky.

13 MON DECEMBER

14 TUE DECEMBER

15 WED DECEMBER

16 THU DECEMBER

DECEMBER FRI **17**

DECEMBER SAT **18**

DECEMBER SUN **19**

NOTES

20 MON DECEMBER

21 TUE DECEMBER

22 WED DECEMBER

23 THU DECEMBER

DECEMBER FRI **24**

DECEMBER SAT **25**

DECEMBER SUN **26**

NOTES

DECEMBER

M	T	W	T	F	S	S
			1	2	3	4	5
6	7	8	9	10	11	12
13	14	15	16	17	18	19
20	21	22	23	24	25	26
27	28	29	30	31		

FUCHSIA GUM
Eucalyptus forrestiana subsp. *dolichorhyncha*
Grows north of Esperance, Western Australia.
Flowers summer.

Eucalyptus forrestiana
Fuchsia Gum

Philippa Nikulinsky '98

27 MON DECEMBER

28 TUE DECEMBER

29 WED DECEMBER

30 THU DECEMBER

DECEMBER FRI 3**1**

JANUARY SAT **1**

JANUARY SUN **2**

NOTES

3 MON JANUARY

4 TUE JANUARY

5 WED JANUARY

6 THU JANUARY

NOTES

2000 YEAR PLANNER

	January	February	March	April	May	June
Mon					1	
Tue		1			2	
Wed		2	1		3	
Thu		3	2		4	1
Fri		4	3		5	2
Sat	1	5	4	1	6	3
Sun	2	6	5	2	7	4
Mon	3	7	6	3	8	5
Tue	4	8	7	4	9	6
Wed	5	9	8	5	10	7
Thu	6	10	9	6	11	8
Fri	7	11	10	7	12	9
Sat	8	12	11	8	13	10
Sun	9	13	12	9	14	11
Mon	10	14	13	10	15	12
Tue	11	15	14	11	16	13
Wed	12	16	15	12	17	14
Thu	13	17	16	13	18	15
Fri	14	18	17	14	19	16
Sat	15	19	18	15	20	17
Sun	16	20	19	16	21	18
Mon	17	21	20	17	22	19
Tue	18	22	21	18	23	20
Wed	19	23	22	19	24	21
Thu	20	24	23	20	25	22
Fri	21	25	24	21	26	23
Sat	22	26	25	22	27	24
Sun	23	27	26	23	28	25
Mon	24	28	27	24	29	26
Tue	25	29	28	25	30	27
Wed	26		29	26	31	28
Thu	27		30	27		29
Fri	28		31	28		30
Sat	29			29		
Sun	30			30		
Mon	31					
Tue						

January	February	March	April	May	June

2000 YEAR PLANNER

July	August	September	October	November	December	
						Mon
	1					Tue
	2			1		Wed
	3			2		Thu
	4	1		3	1	Fri
1	5	2		4	2	Sat
2	6	3	1	5	3	Sun
3	7	4	2	6	4	Mon
4	8	5	3	7	5	Tue
5	9	6	4	8	6	Wed
6	10	7	5	9	7	Thu
7	11	8	6	10	8	Fri
8	12	9	7	11	9	Sat
9	13	10	8	12	10	Sun
10	14	11	9	13	11	Mon
11	15	12	10	14	12	Tue
12	16	13	11	15	13	Wed
13	17	14	12	16	14	Thu
14	18	15	13	17	15	Fri
15	19	16	14	18	16	Sat
16	20	17	15	19	17	Sun
17	21	18	16	20	18	Mon
18	22	19	17	21	19	Tue
19	23	20	18	22	20	Wed
20	24	21	19	23	21	Thu
21	25	22	20	24	22	Fri
22	26	23	21	25	23	Sat
23	27	24	22	26	24	Sun
24	28	25	23	27	25	Mon
25	29	26	24	28	26	Tue
26	30	27	25	29	27	Wed
27	31	28	26	30	28	Thu
28		29	27		29	Fri
29		30	28		30	Sat
30			29		31	Sun
31			30			Mon
			31			Tue

July August September October November December

1998 CALENDAR

JANUARY

M	T	W	T	F	S	S
			1	2	3	4
5	6	7	8	9	10	11
12	13	14	15	16	17	18
19	20	21	22	23	24	25
26	27	28	29	30	31	

FEBRUARY

M	T	W	T	F	S	S
						1
2	3	4	5	6	7	8
9	10	11	12	13	14	15
16	17	18	19	20	21	22
23	24	25	26	27	28	

MARCH

M	T	W	T	F	S	S
						1
2	3	4	5	6	7	8
9	10	11	12	13	14	15
16	17	18	19	20	21	22
23	24	25	26	27	28	29
30	31					

APRIL

M	T	W	T	F	S	S
	1	2	3	4	5	
6	7	8	9	10	11	12
13	14	15	16	17	18	19
20	21	22	23	24	25	26
27	28	29	30			

MAY

M	T	W	T	F	S	S
				1	2	3
4	5	6	7	8	9	10
11	12	13	14	15	16	17
18	19	20	21	22	23	24
25	26	27	28	29	30	31

JUNE

M	T	W	T	F	S	S
1	2	3	4	5	6	7
8	9	10	11	12	13	14
15	16	17	18	19	20	21
22	23	24	25	26	27	28
29	30					

JULY

M	T	W	T	F	S	S
	1	2	3	4	5	
6	7	8	9	10	11	12
13	14	15	16	17	18	19
20	21	22	23	24	25	26
27	28	29	30	31		

AUGUST

M	T	W	T	F	S	S
					1	2
3	4	5	6	7	8	9
10	11	12	13	14	15	16
17	18	19	20	21	22	23
24	25	26	27	28	29	30
31						

SEPTEMBER

M	T	W	T	F	S	S
	1	2	3	4	5	6
7	8	9	10	11	12	13
14	15	16	17	18	19	20
21	22	23	24	25	26	27
28	29	30				

OCTOBER

M	T	W	T	F	S	S
			1	2	3	4
5	6	7	8	9	10	11
12	13	14	15	16	17	18
19	20	21	22	23	24	25
26	27	28	29	30	31	

NOVEMBER

M	T	W	T	F	S	S
						1
2	3	4	5	6	7	8
9	10	11	12	13	14	15
16	17	18	19	20	21	22
23	24	25	26	27	28	29
30						

DECEMBER

M	T	W	T	F	S	S
	1	2	3	4	5	6
7	8	9	10	11	12	13
14	15	16	17	18	19	20
21	22	23	24	25	26	27
28	29	30	31			

2000 CALENDAR

JANUARY

M	T	W	T	F	S	S
					1	2
3	4	5	6	7	8	9
10	11	12	13	14	15	16
17	18	19	20	21	22	23
24	25	26	27	28	29	30
31						

FEBRUARY

M	T	W	T	F	S	S
	1	2	3	4	5	6
7	8	9	10	11	12	13
14	15	16	17	18	19	20
21	22	23	24	25	26	27
28	29					

MARCH

M	T	W	T	F	S	S
		1	2	3	4	5
6	7	8	9	10	11	12
13	14	15	16	17	18	19
20	21	22	23	24	25	26
27	28	29	30	31		

APRIL

M	T	W	T	F	S	S
					1	2
3	4	5	6	7	8	9
10	11	12	13	14	15	16
17	18	19	20	21	22	23
24	25	26	27	28	29	30

MAY

M	T	W	T	F	S	S
1	2	3	4	5	6	7
8	9	10	11	12	13	14
15	16	17	18	19	20	21
22	23	24	25	26	27	28
29	30	31				

JUNE

M	T	W	T	F	S	S
			1	2	3	4
5	6	7	8	9	10	11
12	13	14	15	16	17	18
19	20	21	22	23	24	25
26	27	28	29	30		

JULY

M	T	W	T	F	S	S
					1	2
3	4	5	6	7	8	9
10	11	12	13	14	15	16
17	18	19	20	21	22	23
24	25	26	27	28	29	30
31						

AUGUST

M	T	W	T	F	S	S
	1	2	3	4	5	6
7	8	9	10	11	12	13
14	15	16	17	18	19	20
21	22	23	24	25	26	27
28	29	30	31			

SEPTEMBER

M	T	W	T	F	S	S
				1	2	3
4	5	6	7	8	9	10
11	12	13	14	15	16	17
18	19	20	21	22	23	24
25	26	27	28	29	30	

OCTOBER

M	T	W	T	F	S	S
						1
2	3	4	5	6	7	8
9	10	11	12	13	14	15
16	17	18	19	20	21	22
23	24	25	26	27	28	29
30	31					

NOVEMBER

M	T	W	T	F	S	S
		1	2	3	4	5
6	7	8	9	10	11	12
13	14	15	16	17	18	19
20	21	22	23	24	25	26
27	28	29	30			

DECEMBER

M	T	W	T	F	S	S
				1	2	3
4	5	6	7	8	9	10
11	12	13	14	15	16	17
18	19	20	21	22	23	24
25	26	27	28	29	30	31

ADDRESSES AND TELEPHONE NUMBERS

Name and Address   Telephone

ADDRESSES AND TELEPHONE NUMBERS

Name and Address   Telephone